Honor

Catholics and Cremation Today

H. Richard Rutherford, C.S.C.

A Liturgical Press Book

THE LITURGICAL PRESS
Collegeville, Minnesota

www.litpress.org

Cover design by David Manahan, O.S.B. Photo courtesy of COREL Photos.

The English translation of the texts from the *Order of Christian Funerals* are © 1989, 1995, International Committee on English in the Liturgy, Inc. All rights reserved.

© 2001 by The Order of St. Benedict, Inc., Collegeville, Minnesota. All rights reserved. No part of this booklet may be reproduced in any form or by any means, electronic or mechanical, including photocopying, recording, taping, or any retrieval system, without the written permission of The Liturgical Press, Collegeville, Minnesota 56321. Printed in the United States of America.

2 3 4 5 6 7 8

Library of Congress Cataloging-in-Publication Data

Rutherford, H. Richard.
  Honoring the dead : Catholics and cremation today / H. Richard Rutherford.
    p.   cm.
  Includes bibliographical references.
  ISBN 0-8146-2714-5 (alk. paper)
  1. Cremation—Religious aspects—Christianity. 2. Catholic Church—Doctrines. 3. Catholic Church—Liturgy. I. Title.
BT826.4.R88   2000
264'.020985—dc21
                                                                   00-030651

North American Catholics[1] have discovered cremation. In the 1980s the Cremation Association of North America (CANA) reported the percentage of cremations nationally in the United States hovered around 13 percent, while Canadians recorded nearly 25 percent; by the year 2000 those figures doubled. In the final decades of the last century, Catholics made up an estimated 18 percent of those Americans who chose cremation over interment.[2] As we moved toward the new millennium, this trend continued. In 1997, the U.S. Bishops' Committee on the Liturgy estimated about 20 percent of Catholic funerals involved cremation.[3] In some communities that number approached 50 percent. Today most North American Catholics take the cremation option for granted.

How does cremation affect the Catholic funeral? The *Order of Christian Funerals*[4] professes our heritage and offers an approach to pastoral practice at the time of death that is both authentically Catholic and North American. Although interment of the deceased body in a recognized cemetery remains the preferred Catholic form of final disposition, cremation, followed by a respectful manner of preserving the cremated remains in a place of memorial, is authorized.[5] How we care for a person's mortal remains following cremation is new to the tradition and deserves its own new place in the rituals of American Catholic life.[6]

Heritage

The revised Funeral Liturgy embodies the age-old Christian tradition that the death of a member of our faith community is a spiritual, even sacramental, event. In union with the whole Church, Catholic bereaved bring their deceased loved ones to their final place of rest in a spirit of loving care. Today the choice for cremation by Roman Catholics has found a place within this tradition.

All the same, traditional Catholic funeral rites with the body hold a place of preference. Why has the body of the deceased Christian been so important? The mystery of the incarnation, embracing the life, death, and resurrection of Jesus, is at the center of the Christian belief about death. Also at the center of the Christian way of death is the conviction that our bodies take part in this incarnational faith, which includes liturgical markings throughout our sacramental lifetime. We continue to bathe the body in the waters of baptism, nourish it at the eucharistic banquet, and join it in marriage to another person's body as sacrament of God's presence. At death, from biblical times, we have honored the body as witness among us to the sacramental presence of God and as once a temple of God's Holy Spirit. So too we bring the bodies of our dead into the Funeral Liturgy, a sacramental encounter with the living God through the body of Christ, dead and risen.

Certainly, many who have marked the death of a loved one by means of cremation describe funeral services with the ashes in place of the deceased body as personally satisfying. Without gainsaying those meaningful experiences, we recognize that dying involves our whole person, and that means our bodies, too. The body of a deceased Christian in our midst confronts us with our own mortality, and, ultimately, our utter dependence on God. What we see before us is death's totally destructive power—often harsh and always tangibly real. No life! On the other hand, what Christian liturgy proclaims is hope, founded on the belief that the God of the living—not death—has the last word for us, "*Resurrexit!* He is risen!"

Humanly speaking as well, the deceased body and cremated human remains do not have the same meaning in the symbolism of death. Imagine for a moment that Princess Diana had been cremated immediately after the fatal automobile accident in Paris and then her ashes flown home to

England for a state-funeral. Surely it would have been a memorable funeral, but it would have been different. For millions of people who attended or watched on television, the coffin containing Diana's body, carried in solemn procession and resting center aisle in Westminster Abbey during the Funeral Liturgy, told the world like no other could that Princess Diana was dead.[7] Gathered around that coffin, as it were, people everywhere saw and heard and mourned her death. This is not a matter of right or wrong, better or worse choices; it is simply a matter of difference.

This "difference" explains why for so long the Holy See and the United States Bishops' Conference discouraged bringing the cremated remains into church for the funeral Mass and final commendation. Following the tradition that the Catholic funeral honored the human body as symbol, the Congregation for Sacraments and Divine Worship in 1977 expressed an opinion (a response to a *dubium*) about rites for cremated remains. With Christian anthropology and psychology of ritual as point of departure, the Congregation stated, "It does not seem suitable to celebrate with the ashes present the rite which is intended to honor the body of the dead. This is . . . to respect the integrity of the signs within the liturgical action. . . . The body, not the ashes, receives liturgical honors since it was made the temple of the Spirit of God in baptism. It is important to respect the verity of the sign in order that the liturgical catechesis and the celebration itself be authentic and fruitful."[8]

Although this statement was simply a response by the Holy See to a query and not an authentic interpretation,[9] two of its insights remain instructive today. First, the principle of *liturgical integrity* (signs correspond to the reality they intend to express)[10] is fundamental to good funeral liturgy. The body that participated integrally in all the other expressions of sacramental life is the primary object of liturgical attention in the traditional Funeral Liturgy. In the

5

second place, the letter did not address celebration of all liturgical rites with cremated remains, but specifically "the rite which is intended to honor the body of the dead." This response did not discourage national conferences of bishops from developing funeral rites appropriate to the new symbol of cremated remains. By the late 1990s, however, funerary practice among Catholics in the United States and Canada urged the bishops to recommend an adaptation to the *Order of Christian Funerals* that opted for celebrating one Funeral Liturgy in the presence of both body and cremated remains.[11] All the same, our long Catholic heritage and the complex developments of recent decades joined to recommend a properly Catholic approach to the Funeral Liturgy in an age of cremation.

In sum, how can the heritage of Christian faith at death, with its emphasis on the mystery of Christ's incarnation and resurrection, inform Catholic practice in the use of cremation? It invites us to keep two thoughts in mind. First, in their response to pastoral needs arising from the desire for Funeral Liturgy following cremation, both the U.S. and Canadian Conferences of Bishops reaffirmed Christian faith in face of death, whatever form our mortal remains take—whether corpse or remains recovered in war time or bone fragments following cremation or any other. Thus they aspired to claim due Christian respect for all mortal remains as the final form of the flesh and blood person who lived and died and will rise in relationship with God. Second, when cremated mortal remains take the place of the body in the Catholic Funeral Liturgy, the traditional Catholic funeral which centers on the deceased human body as symbol remains the normative guide for pastoral liturgical practice.

Why did the Catholic Church change its mind about cremation? To situate cremation today in this larger theological picture, some brief historical remarks are in order. In May 1963 the Holy See lifted the prohibition forbidding

Catholics to choose cremation. The forceful and restrictive opposition to cremation in the former Code of Canon Law (c. 1203) did not address cremation as such but opposed the reasons used to justify it, such as burning bodies in an attempt to discredit belief in the resurrection of the dead. These were sectarian, hateful, and contrary to Catholic doctrine.[12] Lifting the prohibition reflected the reality that the anti-Catholic stand responsible for it had disappeared, and the growing practice of cremation in Great Britain and Europe required pastoral attention. Consequently, the option to select cremation as a means of final disposition, following the full Funeral Liturgy with the body present, had been incorporated in the 1983 revision of the Code of Canon Law of (c. 1176) and in Catholic funeral rites (*The Rite of Funerals* [1970–1989]). According to the revised law, good will among the faithful is presumed. Cremation and interment both are subject to the same criterion: that we allow Catholic faith and liturgical practice to guide and direct our pastoral choices.

Where, then, does cremation fit into the Catholic funeral? Practically speaking, this question is peculiarly North American. In Europe and the British Isles, where cremation is widespread, it is incorporated into the Funeral Liturgy as one form of final disposition along with interment (burial in the earth), entombment, or burial at sea. For Catholics in Western countries outside North America, therefore, the body of the deceased person remains the central symbol of the funeral. Cremation has its place in the Rite of Committal, after celebration of the full Funeral Liturgy with the body present.[13] Quite simply, in those cultures, cremation is *an alternative to traditional forms of disposition*.

In the United States and Canada cremation came into vogue not as alternative to other forms of disposition, but as a secular *alternative to the traditional funeral itself*. That is, customary funeral services in the presence of the body of the deceased, described as the "American way of death," became the object of a popular protest, and "immediate" or "direct" cremation at death took its place. Funeral services in the presence of the body gave way to "memorial services" to be held after cremation, with or without the cremated remains present.[14] Both the funeral service and cemetery industries responded by seeking ways to incorporate cremation into their array of goods and services.[15]

This complex situation caused widespread confusion among Catholics. In the early years after Vatican II the U.S. and Canadian Bishops attempted to follow the pattern set out officially in the liturgical documents and the Code of Canon Law: cremation after the funeral with the body, according to the European model. Unofficially, however, large numbers of Catholic faithful began to follow the example of their friends and neighbors: having cremation first and then a "memorial service." The logical Catholic memorial service was, of course, the Mass. Thus a new unofficial liturgical category was born, the so-called "Memorial Mass." Confusion escalated, resulting in pastoral tension between the official and unofficial positions about whether cremated remains could be present at a "Memorial Mass." More on this service below.

Meanwhile throughout the 1980s something else was happening. In contrast to the secular cremation movement and its protest against funeral services with the body, North American Catholics clearly wanted to have both cremation and the full Funeral Liturgy. Cultural and liturgical change was underway.

By 1984 French- and English-speaking bishops in Canada had secured permission from the Holy See to celebrate the full *Funeral Liturgy with the ashes present*. So, when the Canadian bishops published the *Order of Christian Funerals* for use in Canada (1990), it included a minimal rite for "Funeral liturgy in the presence of ashes."[16] Although the 1989 U.S. edition of the *Order of Christian Funerals* included prayers for cremated remains at the Rite of Committal (following the European model), it did not directly address the issue of funeral Mass with the cremated remains. Neither initiating preparation of a special funeral liturgy for cremation nor requesting an exception to universal liturgical law seemed opportune at that time.[17] Nevertheless, the increasing choice for cremation among Catholics in North America was no longer simply a matter of an alternate form of final disposition; it had become "cremation American style," an alternate form of the funeral itself, and seemed to require a liturgy of its own. In 1996, therefore, the National Conference of Catholic Bishops in the United States resolved to request an "indult" to permit celebration of the Catholic Funeral Liturgy with the cremated remains in place of the body. The Holy See authorized the permission on March 21, 1997,[18] and an Appendix to the U.S. *Order of Christian Funerals* (411–438) appeared later that year. Soon thereafter Canadian bishops took the same decision.[19] By the end of the century, Roman Catholics in North America thus took their place in the annals of liturgical history.

In the context of this recent history, we remember that a choice for cremation does not limit one to "immediate cremation" at death. The published cremation Appendix to both Canadian and U.S. editions of funeral rites and their respective catechetical pamphlets restate the official Catholic preference that cremation should follow the Funeral Liturgy, with the Rite of Committal as its proper liturgical setting.

Approach

Although immersed in a culture that values immediate or direct cremation soon after death, Catholics in the United States desire an approach to the use of cremation that is both Catholic and responsive to the personal decisions of the faithful who select cremation for themselves or their loved ones. It seeks the middle ground between exaggerations in our culture that consider funeral rites in any form as all but worthless and, on the other hand, a counter-cultural position that sees the human body of the deceased as the only object of funeral rites. This middle ground is one of ongoing discovery founded on a genuine commitment to inculturation. The 1997 Cremation Appendix to the *Order of Christian Funerals* reflects such an approach. It offers three options.

1) *When cremation takes place following the Funeral Liturgy* (*OCF*, 418–421).

The first option states the traditional preference clearly, proposing that cremation follow the funeral as an alternative to burial of the body while retaining reverent disposition of the cremated remains through burial or entombment in a cemetery. As noted above, this preference is founded on deep Catholic belief in our participation in the mystery of the incarnation and paschal death and resurrection of Jesus. God worked our salvation by becoming one of us, human flesh and blood: he suffered and died as one of us; his crucified body was buried; and he rose from the dead victorious over the power of death to destroy ultimately. We believe we are saved as human persons, who are body and soul, and we look forward in hope to risen life with God in body and soul (Rom 6:3-5). It is not surprising, therefore, that "[T]he Church clearly prefers and urges that the body of the deceased be present for the funeral rites, since the presence of the human body better expresses the values which the Church affirms in those rites."[20]

One way Catholics can opt for the cost benefit of cremation and still celebrate the Funeral Liturgy with the body before cremation combines the selection of embalming with the use of a simple casket. Beyond the familiar plain wooden coffin or simple cloth-covered casket and the ever-increasing option for casket purchase via direct sales and the Internet, manufacturers also provide an appropriately simple shell or "ceremonial" casket. This is, in effect, an outer frame or shell containing a removable inner box, appointed with traditional lining and pillow. The inner box is purchased for final disposition of the deceased; the bereaved ordinarily rent the outer casket frame from a funeral director. Upon completion of the liturgy in the church and the rite of committal at cemetery or crematory,[21] the inner box is removed from the temporary casket for cremation.

By using such a "ceremonial" casket, the Funeral Liturgy honors the body of the deceased present in the midst of the community at a reduced cost, while allowing for cremation as a manner of final disposition. Although somewhat cumbersome in practice and not very popular, this is an economical option to provide for cremation following the Funeral Liturgy with the body. Perhaps it is time the parish or Catholic cemetery consider purchasing this kind of shell casket or coffin, to be able to make such an option more readily available. It is certainly one practical way we can promote the value of celebrating the Catholic funeral with the body of the deceased in a cost-effective manner before cremation.

2) *When cremation and committal take place before the Funeral Liturgy (OCF, 422–425).*

Another option acknowledges situations where cremation and committal both take place before the funeral Mass. Implicitly this option more explicitly acknowledges the distinction between the body and cremated remains as two different forms of mortal remains. That is, it identifies the Rite of Committal as the existing service already designated for use with cremated remains and invites the bereaved to adapt Prayers after Death and the Vigil for the Deceased also to the new circumstances (OCF, 422). Besides adapting these prayers and the vigil for celebration with cremated remains, this option provides a way to maintain traditional attention to the body before cremation. In the latter case, the bereaved can take advantage of the time with the body immediately following the death, which becomes a very special, sacred moment. The reverence and respect for the body and its sacramental character in our faith life ought not be diminished by the choice for immediate cremation and Funeral Liturgy with cremated remains.

Such new cultural circumstances also call for a new liturgical response. Rites of reverence at death have their place in both the *Order of Christian Funerals* and *Anointing and Pastoral Care of the Sick,* beginning not with the funeral or its liturgy but with death. Both these ritual manuals open their models for liturgical pastoral care at the time of death with prayer and ritual gesture directed toward the body. In this present case, drawing on earlier Christian tradition, those who felt so called and moved might participate in a simple ritual of caring for the body soon after death. Caring attention to the deceased body might be expressed, for example, through a tender bathing and dressing of the deceased soon after death, surrounded by prayer, reconciliation, and personal stories. After such a washing and dressing rite, the Rite of Committal of the body with Final Commendation would be appropriate (*OCF,* 422). Such rites attending to the body before cremation would be a welcome expression in preparing the body for the traditional funeral as well.[22]

It should also be noted that this second option reverses the ordinary sequence of funeral rites by suggesting that the bereaved gather for the committal of the cremated remains at a cemetery first, and then proceed to the celebration of the Funeral Liturgy at church (*OCF,* 423).

Sometimes the question arises whether Mass without the body is really a "funeral Mass." The Eucharist celebrated with the bereaved and the deceased's community in the context of the funeral process deserves to be considered a proper "funeral Mass" whether or not the body is present. In other words, Mass celebrated in the funeral context of leave-taking proper to the *Order of Christian Funerals* is a funeral Mass.[23]

What then is a "Memorial Mass"? As we noted above, this term reflects general memorial services, frequently implying a certain span of time after final disposition and so came to connote Mass celebrated primarily in the context of post-funeral memorialization rather than funeral itself. Traditionally Masses on the thirtieth day after death (sometimes termed the "month's mind") and on the anniversary would have been memorial Masses. In the context of the funeral experience of loss and bereavement we should not limit an appreciation of the celebration *par excellence* of the paschal mystery of Jesus at the death of a Christian because of the manner of final disposition one chooses. As long as cremation is selected in good faith, even if outside the normal sequence of funeral rites, Mass celebrated in that context is experienced by the faithful as a true funeral Mass.

This option of reversing the ordinary sequence of funeral rites is founded on the principle that the three parts (or stations) of the *Order of Christian Funerals* may, for pastoral reasons, be celebrated independently of each other. The ordinary sequence of Vigil, Funeral Liturgy, and Committal follows the natural pattern of the human experience following death, marking with appropriate rites three blocks of time (a waking time between death and leave-taking, a time of leave-taking, and a time of final disposition and bereavement beyond). Yet, when the circumstances of the death or other contingencies do not correspond to the natural pattern, such as with the choice for immediate cremation, the three ritual units may move to accommodate the new circumstances.

3) *Funeral Liturgy in the presence of the cremated remains* (*OCF*, 426–431).

Before we turn to a discussion of Funeral Liturgy, including the funeral Mass, with cremated remains, *two preliminary observations* may be helpful. First, the state of corporeal remains (whether lost at sea, destroyed by fire, naturally decomposed in the earth or tomb, or cremated) in no way affects Christian belief in the resurrection of the dead or our recognition in faith and liturgy that we are mortal creatures and death is real. For Catholics, this has been the clearly articulated teaching of the Church throughout the history of cremation in modern times.

Second, times and cultures change.[24] To their credit North American Catholics, immersed in a culture that prefers to streamline funeral rites or reject them all together, have held firm to their sacramental sense that the deceased of the community deserve a funeral, whether the body is present or has been cremated. Memorial services after the fact, characteristic of the new "American way of death," do not fully satisfy people for whom funerals and cemeteries have played such a large role in their Catholic way of life and faith.

In a 1996 interview, Bishop Donald Trautman, then chair of the U.S. Bishops' Committee on the Liturgy, said it best. He told reporters that when cremation takes place immediately following death, it is better to celebrate all the rites of passage with the cremated remains present and not to exclude the remains from the funeral liturgy. In other words, the option to choose immediate or direct cremation is not a rejection of Catholic funeral rites, including the funeral Mass.[25]

This third option, *Funeral Liturgy in the presence of the cremated remains,* therefore, responds best to the practical realities of direct or immediate cremation in the United States and Canada. This includes the understanding that the Rite of Committal would mark the burial or entombment of the remains at an appropriate time following the Funeral Liturgy. It is worth repeating that the widespread choice for immediate cremation was the situation that led the bishops in North America to seek approval from the Holy See for the adaptations to the *Order of Christian Funerals* currently in use.

Liturgical changes: minor but important. Both option two above (adapting the sequence of rites to pastoral circumstances) and the present option of celebrating the Funeral Liturgy with cremated remains in place of the body involve only minor explicit changes in the rites.

First, preparing funeral rites in situations of cremation requires special attention to *language*. The Cremation Appendix adjusts the language of the *Order of Christian Funerals* so that "[p]rayers which do not make reference to the honoring or burying of the body of the deceased should be chosen instead of those which have these themes" (*OCF,* 423 and 428). In some cases, the lists of alternative texts and prayers in the *Order of Christian Funerals* (397–407) will be adequate; in others, ministers must prepare carefully for the special circumstances.

The second adjustment pertains to *ritual actions*. As stated earlier, the decision to celebrate the rites of the *Order of Christian Funerals* in the presence of cremated remains in the same manner as with the body does not introduce new rites for cremation. Here rather, the change is subtle, affecting how one handles cremated remains ritually.

For example, what does a liturgical procession with an urn or other container look like? Who carries them? What arrangements do we need to consider for their placement in the liturgy? On what kind of stand? What are appropriate ways to sprinkle or incense vessels holding cremated remains? What happens to them at the end of the liturgy? How are they cared for during periods of reception immediately following the liturgy? Who will be responsible for their reverent burial or entombment? These are some of the questions to be addressed when adapting the traditional Funeral Liturgy for celebration with cremated remains. The Appendix to the *Order of Christian Funerals,* including adaptations for the celebration of the Funeral Liturgy in the presence of cremated remains, and the excellent catechetical pamphlet *Reflections on the Body, Cremation, and Catholic Funeral Rites,* offer some initial suggestions to encourage reception of the adaptations.

In the first place, the section on *Funeral Liturgy in the presence of cremated remains* directs that "[t]he cremated remains of the body are to be placed in a worthy vessel" and "a small table or stand is to be prepared for them in the place normally occupied by the coffin" (*OCF,* 427). Some planning is necessary for this etiquette of the Funeral Liturgy with cremated remains to flow smoothly.

What about placement of the cremated remains in the liturgy? The rubric about placing a small stand or table at the place normally occupied by the coffin pertains to placement during the Funeral Liturgy. But how do they get there? "The vessel containing the cremated remains may be carried to its place in the entrance procession or may be placed on this table or stand sometime before the liturgy begins" (*OCF,* 427). The latter option requires no further explanation. However, when cremated remains are to be part of the rite of reception, pastoral practice with the cremation adaptations suggests that a second table be available at the place of reception to facilitate the sprinkling rite. Although it is liturgically appropriate to sprinkle the container of cremated remains while it is being held by a member of the funeral party, the size of container and the arrangement of participants often make such a ritual seem awkward and elicits inopportune snickers. In such situations, sprinkling the cremated remains sometimes inadvertently splashes unintended amounts of holy water on participants' clothes and, what's worse, on their makeup. A simple table, covered with an appropriate cloth, allows the funeral party (and the larger community as well, when possible) to stand around the vessel with cremated remains as they would a coffin and provides space for the minister to carry out the sprinkling rite with due decorum.

A further question involves how the cremated remains get to the church in the first place. The answer seems simple. Of course, the funeral director brings them—just like the body. That is true when the bereaved have made arrangements with a traditional funeral home to handle the cremation and take part in the funeral. However, as discussed above, people often choose cremation precisely to simplify the cost of such traditional funeral customs. Depending on the kind of services arranged with the cremation provider and keeping in mind the particular reasons for selecting cremation (especially where cost has been a factor), one must determine how the cremated remains will find their way to the church or place of disposition.

The simplest solution is to have a member of the funeral party collect the container with cremated remains from the crematorium or funeral service provider shortly before the funeral and bring it with them to the liturgy. In this case be sure to arrange in advance with the provider holding the cremated remains what will be needed by way of authorization to release them.

A second possibility is to have the cremation provider deliver them to the parish, if delivery is part of their service package. (Frequently they will be mailed; UPS and FedEx prohibit shipping cremated remains.) Of course, it is important to arrange with the parish that the cremated remains will arrive before the liturgy. Parishes will have to determine how to keep them until the funeral. If the time is short and the church secure or with someone present to keep watch, they may be placed in advance in the place where they will be during the liturgy. Otherwise, they might be kept in a locked cabinet or other secure place where they will not be disturbed or disturb others.

To simplify all this, when parish instruction on cremation presents the liturgical adaptations involved, it might suggest two patterns corresponding to the liturgy with cremated remains: when the funeral party brings the cremated remains with them, the rite of reception would be celebrated with the cremated remains as part of the reception rite and carried in procession; when the cremated remains are delivered in advance, they would be in their place at the head of the aisle when the party arrives for the funeral. In the latter case, only the funeral party would be received at the door and process with the ministers into the church (*OCF,* 427).

When a person dies and is cremated in one part of the country or world and the funeral will be celebrated in another, the cremated remains will have to be transported long distances. As above, shipment by the U.S. Postal Service is customary, but sometimes people want to accompany the deceased's remains.

What about transport on airplanes? In general, this is a matter of personal choice. While maintaining the principle of respect, one may wrap the container with the cremated remains and send it as accompanying baggage or take it along as carry-on luggage. However, although most states do not regulate the transport of cremated remains, regulations that do exist in some states and in countries abroad vary considerably. For example, in Iowa, cremated remains are to be handled in the same way as other bodies, and in Texas, transport or other activity with the ashes may not exceed thirty days. In short, one should ask the airline office or the State Department of Public Health for specifics about the regions of travel before preparing the cremated remains for transport by air.

What is a "worthy vessel"? At the present time, neither the cremation Appendix nor the U.S. Bishops' Committee on the Liturgy answer the question explicitly. Although pastoral practice will determine that in time, the principle of respect for cremated remains and directives regarding final disposition do give a good sense of the kind of containers to avoid. Thus, jewelry and dishes, statuary and space capsules (to mention only a few examples) are unacceptable in the present adaptations of Catholic funerary custom to cremation, although these are common designer containers in the growing cremation culture.

At issue here is the commercialization of cremation. What began as a movement toward simplicity has spawned ostentatious offspring in the new cremation industry. Will Catholics, whose desire for simplicity and cost-effective funerals created the demand for Funeral Liturgy in the presence of cremated remains, become the consumers of these cremation goods and services? Will religious designer urns, quickly taking their place side by side with the casket in the marketing strategies and status symbols of the American way of death,[26] impact the Catholic spirit of noble simplicity in the revised *OCF*?

What about covering the container of cremated remains with a white pall? The cremation Appendix states simply, "The covering of the cremated remains with a pall is omitted" (*OCF*, 434). This is the only ritual gesture in the cremation adaptations that differentiates cremated remains from the deceased body as two different forms of mortal remains.

The decision to omit the pall in rites with cremated remains was not taken lightly because of the commitment to secure for cremated remains the "same respect given to the human body from which they come" (*OCF*, 417). Yet, in an effort to recognize that they are different from the "corporeal remains of a human body" (*Reflections,* 11), without diminishing due respect, the white pall (with its explicit symbolic association to the human body in the baptismal liturgy) was reserved for Funeral Liturgy with the body present. Not all agree with this decision, but it is believed to be consistent with the intention of the indult granted by Rome and with the U.S. Bishops' reminder that the Church "urges that the body of the deceased be present for the funeral rites, since the presence of the body better expresses the values which the Church affirms in those rites" (*OCF,* 413 and *passim*). Far from diminishing the respect due cremated remains, reserving the pall for funerals with the body present helps us appreciate the human reality of the difference as well as the symbolic centrality of the body.

One way of expressing the special character of cremated remains is to provide a unique and worthy vessel for the Funeral Liturgy following cremation. For this reason some parishes are providing their own Christian vessel to contain and carry the remains of the deceased at all celebrations of the Funeral Liturgy in the presence of cremated remains. Not to be limited by the notion of "urn," they have looked to something like a modern "ossuary" or "ark."[27] Historically such "bone boxes" date from a time when it was customary, after a certain period of time, to exhume the remains of the dead and preserve their remaining bone fragments for proper remembrance. Often measuring some 10 x 20 inches or larger and made of stone, they resemble miniature sarcophagi or caskets. From their places in niches in ancient church cemeteries or along cloister walls such ossuaries might be viewed as early forerunners of Christian cremation containers. After all, cremated remains are in fact more bone fragments than ashes.[28]

Prototypes of a modern parish ossuary or ark resemble a small cedar chest. They are large enough to contain the plain cardboard or plastic boxes provided by the crematory as well as urns and other more elaborate containers, and yet not so large as to duplicate a casket. They could be constructed of local materials, such as pine or myrtle wood, local marble, or light-weight terra-cotta, for example. Appropriate Christian symbols could decorate them, perhaps reflecting the salvation iconography of the early catacombs.

Upon arrival at the church, during the rite of reception, members of the funeral party place their personal container of cremated remains inside this parish "ossuary." Or, according to the other proposed option for liturgy with cremated remains, the personal container of cremated remains would already be in place, inside the parish container, at the head of the aisle. The parish vessel has the added advantage of being a worthy vessel, which maintains simplicity and avoids surprises at the choice of container provided.

Furthermore, such an ossuary or ark is a substantial vessel especially fitting for ritual actions such as sprinkling, incensing, and procession. Depending on its size and weight and the weight of its contents, a single "pallbearer" might bear the ossuary in ceremonial fashion, similar to the way that ministers carry the gospel book or gifts in procession. A heavier ossuary might be provided with handles on its ends and two persons might carry it between them in procession. This is an evolving concept, to be sure, but it serves as an example of a "worthy vessel" that reflects an approach to liturgy with cremated remains that is consistent both with the funerary tradition of the Church and the reality of cremation, but does not buy into (figuratively and literally!) the consumerism surrounding it.

Interment or Scattering of Cremated Remains. Finally, a word about the Catholic manner of disposing of cremated remains. Liturgical tradition and the role the Catholic cemetery plays in preserving the memory of Christians profess explicit belief in the promise of resurrection. Hence the clear preference for preserving the remains of our loved ones, whether by interment or in a tomb or columbarium.[29] The cremation Appendix to the *OCF* states,

> The cremated remains should be buried in a grave or entombed in a mausoleum or columbarium. The practice of scattering cremated remains on the sea, from the air, or on the ground, or keeping cremated remains in the home of a relative or friend of the deceased are not the reverent disposition that the Church requires (*OCF*, 417).[30]

One respected Catholic cemetery director suggests the following effective rule of thumb to guide the bereaved and practitioners alike.

> A method to test the appropriateness of memorialization options is to ask: "What is the parallel to full body memorialization . . . ?" For example, there are alternatives currently available or being planned which encourage family members to take a portion of the cremated remains of the body home in the form of pottery, glassware, and statuary. I can easily imagine an attempt—albeit ill informed—to appeal to Catholic piety by creating "Madonna and Child statues" out of the cremated remains of the body. . . . Now, with each of these examples, and there are certainly others, what are the parallels when it comes to memorialization of a full body? I know of no efforts to market subdivision of corpses, decorative jewelry from portions of the body, or space flights for the "living-impaired". . . . Therefore, while the bishops have not specifically said "No keepsake jewelry," we must understand the purpose of such memorialization. It is to subdivide the cremated remains of the body so that they can be taken home, worn as a necklace, and the like. An argument might be made that this type of memorial in fact meets short-term personal needs of the bereaved. But, does it recognize the public place of the relationship of Christ and his Church with the person who has died?[31]

His point is well grounded in the U.S. Bishops' catechesis,

> The Church's belief in the sacredness of the human body and the resurrection of the dead has traditionally found expression in the care taken to prepare the bodies of the deceased for burial. The prayers and gestures of Catholic funeral rites likewise affirm the Church's reverence for the bodies of its deceased members.
> That reverence is not always shared by the society in which the Church exists. An exaggerated sense of privacy and individualism often prevents family members from providing the custody and care of the body that is properly theirs. . . . These practices contradict the Church's emphasis on the indispensable role of the wider community in the dying and death of a Christian. . . . Catholic tradition urges the Church today to face death with honest rituals that preserve its Christian and human values.[32]

Some have argued in favor of subdividing cremated remains of loved ones as analogous to the Church's long history of dividing and honoring the relics of the saints. If that is acceptable for the relics of martyrs and saints, why not for the cremated remains of holy people today? From my perspective, the consistent teaching of the Catholic Church in modern times (from the Council of Trent through Vatican II to the present) offers a twofold answer. In the first place, the Church has reserved the veneration of relics exclusively for canonized saints of the universal Christian calendar. Second, every effort has been made to curb past abuses in the traffic of relics. Forms of memorialization that would be considered an abuse in the veneration of saints' relics would not be "the reverent disposition that the Church requires" for the cremated remains of deceased Catholics.[33]

This cemetery director's words of wisdom from the field conclude with the awareness that people's values, attitudes,

23

and beliefs are changing and make it difficult to prepare for tomorrow. "In meeting the needs of Catholic families who choose cremation," he asserts, "I remind you again: Appropriate cremation memorialization for Catholic families will:

1. Respect the Church's understanding of the human person;

2. Reflect the Church's teaching on the relationship created at baptism between the Christian, God, and the community of believers;

3. And, cremation memorialization will take place within the context of the Catholic perspective on cremation, that is, memorialization that offers a permanent place of dignity, a place set aside and recognized by the community as a place to remember and give thanks. In addition, the life of the Christian is permanently recorded."[34]

Conclusion

One of the best qualities of the new *Order of Christian Funerals* is its ability to be an appropriate expression of Catholic faith at death, even under these newest of circumstances. With sound pastoral judgment, founded on a full appreciation of the *Order of Christian Funerals,* and with commitment to the faith it proclaims, Catholic parishes will serve their people with greater flexibility and inspiration. Once again the liturgy is inviting us to be somewhere none of us has ever been; it is our pastoral responsibility to translate this invitation into living liturgy for an ever-growing number of Catholics who request cremation.

The practice of Catholic churches in countries where cremation has been common for some time offers little direction to the new North American experience. Because funerary customs elsewhere generally do not involve embalming or cosmetic restoration for viewing, and coffins or caskets are unassuming, it makes little difference whether interment or cremation is selected. In practice the Funeral Liturgy at church with the body present is the norm, whether burial or cremation follows.

Nevertheless, where those churches do have considerable experience is with committal rites and, in particular, with the extreme time constraints placed on these rites due to constant demand at crematories. Their advice to national conferences of Catholic bishops who are facing the increased demand for cremation for the first time is to exert all possible influence to ensure adequate time for a worthy celebration of the Funeral Liturgy and committal rites. Has the time arrived for the Catholic cemeteries—especially diocesan cemeteries in larger cities—to have their own crematories? However that may be, it is clear that as Catholic consumers of cremation services we must make our values known if we are to preserve the authentic inculturation of the faith in the twenty-first century.[35] Our heritage and its embodiment in the *Order of Christian Funerals* are a trustworthy guide for Catholics in North America as we address these demands of modern culture.

Yes, North American Catholics have discovered cremation. That will not surprise historians of religion who study our century. At the turn of the next millennium, for example, chroniclers may take note of the latest tragedy to strike the historic Kennedy dynasty in the untimely death of John F. Kennedy, Jr., and his travelling companions. Yet only the most astute reader will recall, I submit, that their Catholic funerals included cremation and the burial of their remains at sea.[36] According to the projections with which this essay opened, many Catholics will continue to espouse the established values of a funeral with the body of the deceased present. At the same time, cremation will be commonplace in the Catholic community. How we respond to the cultural challenge to christen cremation will be among the touchstones whereby future generations measure our fidelity to the Catholic tradition and to the renewal of the Church in the modern world after Vatican II.

―――――――――――――

The addition of "today" to the title of an essay originally conceived over a decade ago has resulted in a complete revision of that earlier edition (*Honoring the Dead: Catholics and Cremation* [Collegeville: The Liturgical Press, 1991]). During those years our culture has changed and so have some of my thoughts about this complex and ever-evolving topic. Together with the Church in North America, I continue to grapple with issues of fidelity and inculturation but stand firm on the fundamental values that take liturgical form in the *Order of Christian Funerals*.

This revision would not have come to light without the competent, painstaking assistance of respected colleagues at both theological and editorial levels. While I take full responsibility for the content as it has taken shape, for their invaluable contributions I am deeply indebted to colleagues and friends Will Deming, Larry Hansen, and Alan J. Helyer.

Notes

[1] Although the practice of cremation in Mexico is changing, "North America" in this essay refers chiefly to the United States and Canada. Nevertheless, the consideration of Catholic principles generally applies to Mexico as well. See the *Ritual de Exequias Cristianas* (1994) with its Appendix on cremation.

[2] Center for Gerontological Education Research and Services (GERAS), "Project Understanding," organized by Grace Dawson and reported in Rebecca Voelker, "As Old as Fire," *Notre Dame Magazine* 16 (1987) 12–14. See also Grace D. Dawson, John F. Santos, and David C. Burdick, "Differences in Final Arrangements Between Burial and Cremation as the Method of Body Disposition," *Omega* 21 (1990) 129–46, and Joe A. Adams, *Project Understanding: A National Survey of Cremation* (Evanston, Ill.: National Research and Information Center, 1986).

[3] Committee on the Liturgy, National Conference of Catholic Bishops, *Reflections on the Body, Cremation and Catholic Funeral Rites* (Washington, D.C.: United States Catholic Conference, 1997) 8.

[4] National Conference of Catholic Bishops, *Order of Christian Funerals*, 1989. Available from three publishers: Catholic Book Publishing Co., The Liturgical Press, and Liturgy Training Publications.

[5] Ibid., 416–17.

[6] According to the *OCF* "Funeral Liturgy" designates Catholic funeral rites centered on the celebrating of a funeral Mass, ordinarily at the (parish) church, with the body present. When Mass is not part of the funeral rites with the body, the *OCF* uses "Funeral Liturgy outside Mass." Terms such as "cremated remains" or "mortal remains" and occasionally "ashes" are preferred to the recently coined industry term "cremains." This liturgical usage is formal and consistent with legislative documents (e.g., State of California, Assembly Bill No. 1705: Cremated Remains) and is distinct from marketing language (e.g., "Creative Cremains" on the website www.creativecremains.com/home.html).

[7] See Mary Dombeck, "Death Rituals and Life Values: The American Way." In Sherman, Anthony F., ed., *Rites of Death and Dying* (Collegeville: The Liturgical Press, 1988) 47–49.

[8] Committee on the Liturgy, National Conference of Catholic Bishops, *Newsletter* 13 (1977) 59.

[9] Some commentators, this author included, assigned greater canonical authority to this explanation than it warranted. See Henchal, Michael J., "Cremation: Canonical Issues," *The Jurist* 55 (1995) 286 (and *passim* for the most comprehensive discussion of both canonical

and pastoral questions arising from cremation at that time). Henchal argues persuasively in support of the canonical option to celebrate the *OCF* in the presence of cremated remains in place of the body—the position affirmed in 1997 by the Roman indult and the U.S. Bishops' Appendix to the *OCF*. This present essay aspires to keep alive the liturgical questions inherent in such major symbol shifts.

[10] Constitution on the Liturgy, n. 7.

[11] By 1997 also the intention of the Roman Congregation in granting the indult, "As regards the question of new liturgical texts, it would seem preferable to limit these in so far as possible to suitable selections and adaptations of existing texts, rather than developing a whole alternative rite." See Committee on the Liturgy, National Conference of Catholic Bishops, *Newsletter* 33 (1997) 14.

[12] Although more than thirty years old and to be read with full awareness of contemporary developments, the best summary of this history is Irion, Paul E., *Cremation* (Philadelphia: Fortress, 1968).

[13] For an insight into the widespread practice of cremation in Great Britain and its impact on pastoral care and liturgy, see Jupp, Peter C., and Tony Rogers, eds., *Interpreting Death: Christian Theology and Pastoral Practice* (London and Washington: Cassell, 1997).

[14] See, for example, the revised and posthumously published classic: Jessica Mitford, *The American Way of Death Revisited* (New York: Knopf, 1998).

[15] Examples span the final decade of the twentieth century, from the cover of National Funeral Directors Association trade journal, *The Director* (cover and lead article, November 1991) to the January 2000 issue of *American Cemetery* with its look back at some 1988 predictions by fellow cemeterians. "We need change. We need to concentrate on meaningful memorialization of cremated remains, not resisting cremation. Our urns should be better, more expressive and, yes, more expensive. Our niches should be more the focus of memorialization. . . . We should be planning more—bigger—better columbaria for the inurnment of more—bigger—better urns. The small cube-like urn . . . should give way to the meaningful memorialization that consumers will accept once value has been established" (*The American Cemetery,* January 2000, 22). See also *The Director,* July 2000, *passim.*

[16] Canadian Conference of Catholic Bishops (Ottawa: Publications Service, 1990). See Appendix IV, 432–33.

[17] Note the recent history with the *Order of Christian Funerals:* in preparation since the early 1980s, under scrutiny in Rome after approval by the U.S. bishops in 1985, and finally published in 1989.

[18] Prot. N. CD 1589/96/L.

[19] See *Catholics and Cremation: Some answers to questions regarding cremation and funerals.* Canadian Conference of Catholic Bishops, 1998 (www.cccb.ca/english/episdocs.asp).

[20] *Order of Christian Funerals,* Appendix: *Cremation,* n. 413. See also *Reflections,* 7.

[21] Although the ordinary practice in Europe and the United Kingdom, the experience of celebrating the Rite of Committal at a crematory is new to North America. Nevertheless, it is increasing and taking advantage of the Internet to encourage participation, as the following illustrates: "Over the years, families have inquired about visiting [our crematory] to witness the initiation of cremation for a loved one. . . . Many of the families who visited told us how grateful they were to be able to participate. Many indicated that it helped bring closure, which is so important to the survivors. They also expressed that other family members or friends wished to take part, but were unable to attend. . . . For this reason, we created the Cremation-Cam" (*The Director* 71 [1999] 48–50).

[22] See, for example, "Different Symbols—Different Rites: Funeral Liturgy with Cremated Remains" in *Liturgical Ministry* 4 (1995) 39, 43–44.

[23] The earlier criterion that designated Mass followed by the Absolution (now Final Commendation) as "funeral Mass" no longer applies. Since the promulgation of the *Ordo Exsequiarum* of 1969 the rite of Final Commendation stands on its own, independent of the Mass.

[24] Signs of the times include, for example, on-line funerals (www.fergersonfuneralhome.com), cremation services for those unable to attend via Cremation-Cam (www.paradisecrematory.com), virtual cemeteries (www.worldgardens.com), among many such options.

[25] Cited in *Catholic Cemetery* (May 1997) 8.

[26] See, for example, www.urnmall.com by the Internet Cremation Society, where in addition to its five participating companies, some fifty other providers are listed.

[27] An excellent example of this kind of liturgical vessel was designed by Mario Locsin in 1989 for the funeral of Nancy McCormick, wife of Robert E. Rambusch. After the funeral Rambusch donated the ossuary to St. Joseph Roman Catholic Parish, Greenwich Village, N.Y., for which it was designed. Locsin explains his intention that such an ossuary be designed in accord with the liturgical plan and spirit of each parish church. In January 2000 John Vogelpohl of Meyer-Vogelpohl Church Goods & Religious Art offered the first commercial model for sale (Catalog 2000, 1). While the initial cost to a parish of such an ossuary (whether purchased or custom commissioned) is

substantial (ca. $2000), it is a one-time outlay of funds for many years of parish use and, even then, about half the advertised average cost of a casket.

[28] What is the cremation process? The casket or container is placed in the cremation chamber, where the temperature is raised to approximately 1600 degrees to 1800 degrees Fahrenheit. After approximately 2 to $2\,^1/_2$ hours, all organic matter is consumed by heat or evaporation. The residue which is left is bone fragments, known as cremated remains. The cremated remains are then carefully removed from the cremation chamber. Any metal is removed with a magnet and later disposed of in cemetery grounds. The cremated remains are then processed into fine particles and are placed in the container provided by the crematorium or placed in an urn purchased by the family. The entire process takes approximately three hours. Throughout the cremation process, a carefully controlled labeling system ensures correct identification. This data on the technology of cremation and answers to many other cremation questions are available at www.icfa.org/Cremation.htm. See also www.xroads.com/~funerals.

[29] "Columbarium" is defined as a "vault or similar structure with recessed niches in the walls for storing the ashes of the dead," Harrah, Barbara K., and David F. Harrah, *Funeral Service* (Metuchen, N.J.: Scarecrow, 1976) 263. Columbaria have been available at Catholic and other cemeteries for some time. The U.S. Bishops state in *Reflections* (11–12) they "should not be incorporated into parish church buildings." Whether authorization is required to build columbaria outside the church buildings remains a matter of continuing discussion at the beginning of the new millennium. For canonical background on this, see Henchal, op. cit., 296–98.

[30] For further discussion on the interpretation of "scattering," see Henchal, ibid., 293–98.

[31] Address by Richard Peterson, Director, Associate Catholic Cemeteries of the Archdiocese of Seattle, to the Cremation Association of North America: "Cremation Memorialization for the Next 1,000 Years," August 21, 1998.

[32] *Reflections*, 5.

[33] A summary of Catholic teaching in this matter may be found in the Dogmatic Constitution on the Church *(Lumen gentium)* n. 51, the *Code of Canon Law* (1983) cc. 1190 and 1237, and in the *Decretum de invocatione, veneratione et reliquiis Sanctorum, et sacris imaginibus* of the Council of Trent, DS 1822–1825.

[34] Peterson, ibid.

[35] Other voices leave no doubt about their values. Perhaps with tongue in cheek, but nonetheless revealing, is the following 1988

retrospective in the January 2000 issue of *The American Cemetery:* "Burial in the earth will become unfashionable and will ultimately be banned by the federal government in 2030. A new process will make cremation obsolete. 'Crystallization' will reduce the body so that there will be absolutely no trace left whatsoever. . . . A computer software package will take the mourners step by step through the grief therapy process. The only form of memorialization will be a holograph of the 'loved one' that appears on a small object given by the hospital as a token of their appreciation of the business" (*The American Cemetery*, January 2000, 23).

[36] Burial of a vessel containing cremated remains at sea does not seem to be the same as scattering cremated remains over the ocean or other body of water. For a different opinion and further discussion, see Henchal, op. cit., 295–96.